NORTHERN CENTRAL RAILWAY
OF YORK
™

"All Aboard" STARTS WITH A!

WRITTEN BY
ANTHONY D. FREDERICKS

ILLUSTRATED BY
PHYLLIS DISHER FREDERICKS

Welcome to the Northern Central Railway — a journey into history! Along the way, you'll learn all about trains... and have a lot of fun, too. You will meet interesting people, see exciting new sights, and discover things you never knew before. You're in for quite a ride!

Trains are really exciting! Sure, they make lots of noise with their whistles, clickety-clacks, and all that chugging along the rails. But that's what so many people like about them. They're also a fun way to travel — very different from cars or bicycles — and that's something else to like about them. They're also big... a lot bigger than almost any other form of transportation. That's pretty cool!

So, come on board. When you're finished reading this book, you'll know a lot about a very special railroad — the Northern Central Railway of York (NCR). In fact, you will be an official NCR expert!

The adventure is waiting. It's time to turn the page and begin your journey.

All Aboard!

NOTE TO PARENTS & TEACHERS:

There are two open-ended questions (with no right or wrong answers) for each of the 26 NCR features. Use them to start a conversation with your child (or students) and please feel free to add your own questions, too.

"All Aboard! starts with A,"
the conductor yells out loud.
Everybody's in their seats —
a happy cheerful crowd.

When the conductor of a train shouts, "ALL ABOARD!"
it's a signal that the train will leave the station soon.
That's when everyone should be on the train and in their
seats. You don't want to miss this ride, do you?

- What might be some other words a conductor could use besides "ALL ABOARD!"?
- If you could talk to the conductor, what would you like to say?

B is for the bikes
that travel on the Trail.
The bikers wave and smile
at their friends who ride the rail.

NCR trains travel along the Heritage Rail Trail County Park – a path where a second set of railroad tracks once ran. People use this path for walking and biking. Bikers can also have their bikes carried on the train, and then get off and ride them back to where they started.

- What do you like most about riding a bike?
- Why do you think people like to ride bikes along the Trail?

"Clickety Clack" starts with C,
our favorite sound of all.
You hear it all the time —
from springtime through the fall.

WM.H. SIMPSON
YORK

A train makes many different sounds when it's moving along the railroad track. The wheels make clickety-clack sounds on the metal rails, the whistle blows, the engine makes a chug-chug sound, and the coach cars make all sorts of squeaks, rattles, and grinding noises.

- What is your favorite sound in the world?
- Why do you think trains make so much noise?

D is for the Diesel —
a locomotive grand.
It's a large and mighty engine.
Yes, it always takes command!

A diesel engine – named for its inventor, Rudolf Diesel – is a very powerful machine. A diesel locomotive works by compressing air inside the engine. The temperature of the air rises and ignites diesel fuel. This causes pistons to move up and down creating power that moves a train or other form of transportation.

- How is a diesel engine similar to the engine in your parents' car?
- Why do you think the diesel engine on a train is so large?

E is for the Engine

that sends up clouds of steam.
It chugs across the county.
Oh, this journey is a dream!

On many railroads, a steam engine pulls or pushes the train along the track. The power for the engine comes from the burning of coal, oil, or wood (in order to make steam). All that steam eventually comes out of the smokestack. It's quite an impressive sight!

- What are some of the ways you have traveled?
- What are some places (away from home) you and your family have visited?

F is for "Fall Foliage" —
an excursion down the line.
The leaves show brilliant colors.
It's nature's best design!

In the fall, many trees begin to change colors.
Leaves that were once green become red,
yellow, or orange. Soon afterward, the leaves
begin to fall off the trees, becoming a rainbow
of colors on the ground. By next spring,
however, new leaves grow in their place –
bright green again – fluttering beside the
railroad tracks.

- What do you like best about fall?
- What is your favorite fall color?

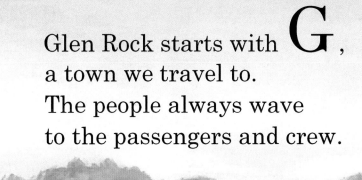

Glen Rock starts with G,
a town we travel to.
The people always wave
to the passengers and crew.

The Glen Rock Express travels from New Freedom to the borough of Glen Rock in southern York County. Glen Rock was founded in 1837 and the first passenger train began service to the town in 1838. The train allowed local farmers to transport their products to Baltimore and York. At one time, dozens of trains came in and out of Glen Rock every day.

- Why are some towns small and others large?
- Why do you think people enjoy living in a small town?

Hanover Junction starts with H.
It's not that far away.
Mister Lincoln once stopped there,
and then went on his way.

The Hanover Junction Railroad Station was built in 1851-1852.
President Abraham Lincoln visited the station on November 18
and 19, 1863, on his way to Gettysburg to give the
Gettysburg Address. On April 21, 1865, President Lincoln's
funeral train also passed through Hanover Junction.

- Look at the illustration on this page. What do you like most
  about the Hanover Junction Railroad Station?
- How is the Hanover Junction Railroad Station similar to,
  or different from, the station in New Freedom?

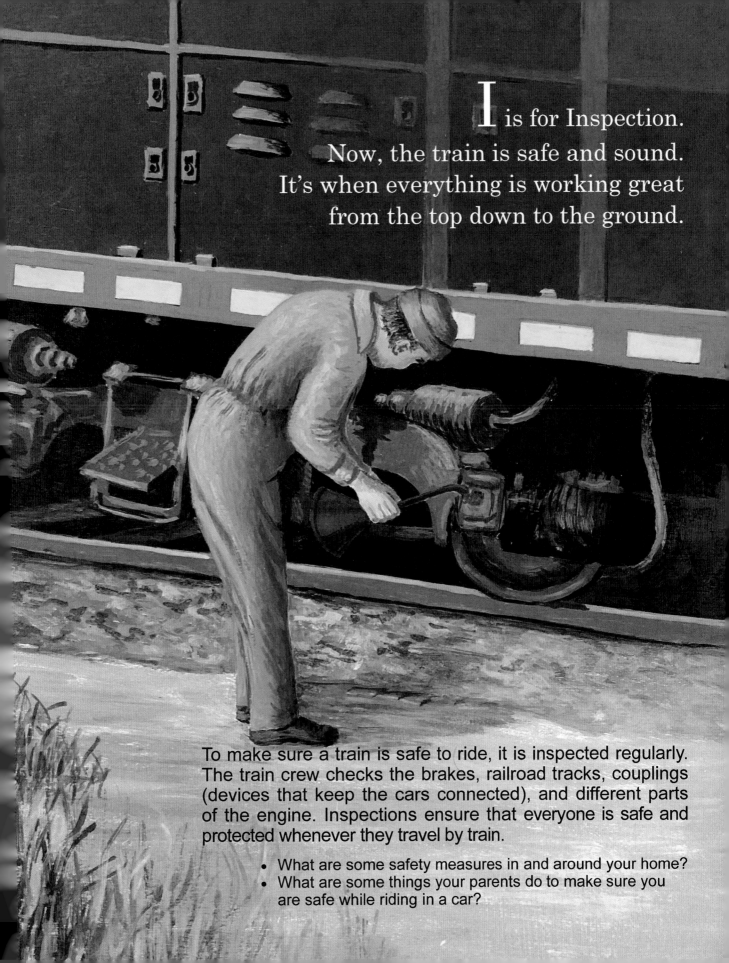

I is for Inspection.
Now, the train is safe and sound.
It's when everything is working great
from the top down to the ground.

To make sure a train is safe to ride, it is inspected regularly.
The train crew checks the brakes, railroad tracks, couplings
(devices that keep the cars connected), and different parts
of the engine. Inspections ensure that everyone is safe and
protected whenever they travel by train.

- What are some safety measures in and around your home?
- What are some things your parents do to make sure you
  are safe while riding in a car?

Journey starts with **J**.
"Steam into History."
The train chugs through the past.
It's exciting – don't you agree?

When the Northern Central Railway of York began in 2013, its first name was "Steam into History." It changed its name several years later, but it is still a journey into the past. It uses authentic rail cars and true-to-life locomotives based on traditional designs. It's a trip, and an adventure, into the history of this country.

- It you could travel back in time, where would you like to go and who would you like to see?
- What do you like most about history?

K is for the knowledge we learn upon the train. The science and the history really fills our brain.

There's lots of stuff to learn when you ride the train. You can learn about how the train works, the various plants and animals you see along the way, the history of the railroad, stories about train travel, and some famous people who have been on the Northern Central Railway of York. Yes, there is a lot to discover!

- What is the most important thing you've learned about trains?
- What would you like to learn about trains that you don't know now?

The library starts with L —
a place that's full of fun,
with train books on the shelves
to share with everyone.

The York County Library System has 13 different libraries throughout the county. Residents of York County can check out books, reserve videos, use computers, search databases, obtain materials from around the country, or just sit and enjoy a good book...like a good train book! Passengers will note that the train passes by the Arthur Hufnagel Public Library of Glen Rock.

- What do you like most about the library?
- Why are libraries important places?

M is for museum —
a place that's really cool.
With lots of things to learn,
it's like a little school.

A museum is a place where artifacts, or items from the past, are on display for visitors to view. There are history museums, dinosaur museums, science museums, and airplane museums (among many others). The Northern Central Railway of York museum at Hanover Junction preserves items (and stories) important in the history of the NCR.

- What would you like most about visiting a museum – especially one devoted to trains?
- If you could start your own museum, what would you put in it?

N is for New Freedom.
It's where the train starts out,
a historic country town,
friendly people all about!

New Freedom is located in the southern part of York County. It was originally known as "Freedom" for the Free family who lived there in the 1800s. However, there was another place with the same name, so the word "New" was added and, ever since 1873, the town has been officially known as New Freedom.

- What do you like most about New Freedom or the New Freedom Railroad Station?
- If you could live anywhere in the world, where would you live? Why?

Overpass starts with O.

The train – a heavy load –
safely passes over
a stream or busy road.

An overpass is like a bridge. (They are sometimes known as trestle bridges.) It allows a train to go up and over a valley, road, street, stream or a river. The train doesn't have to stop – it can continue on its journey without interruption. Some overpasses allow cars or boats to travel underneath the train tracks.

- Where would you find an overpass near where you live?
- What do you think would happen if a train couldn't go over a river?

P is for the passengers
who travel here and there.
They love this expedition —
there's magic everywhere!

People who travel in cars, buses, airplanes, boats, or trains are passengers.
Every time you travel in something that takes you from one place to another,
you are a passenger. When you go to the store in a car, you are a car
passenger. And when you travel on a train, you are a train passenger.

- What do you like most about being a train passenger?
- How many different forms of transportation can you name on which
  you have been a passenger?

Q is for the questions.
It's something we must know,
like "How old is this train?"
or "Why is it going slow?"

People ask questions to learn something new – to discover new information they didn't know before. Teachers often say that students who ask questions are good learners and good thinkers. When we ask questions every day we get a little smarter! By the way, NCR trains travel at a (slow) speed of just 10 MPH for safety reasons.

- What is a question you have about trains?
- How could you find the answer to your question?

R is for the Railway,
a transportation power.
It runs along an old-time track
in sun or rainy shower.

Completed in 1858, the Northern Central Railway connected
Baltimore, Maryland, with Sunbury, Pennsylvania. It ran along
the Susquehanna River and operated for over one hundred
years until 1972. That's when Hurricane Agnes destroyed
much of the track. In 2013, it was revitalized and began its new
life through various towns and sites in York County.

- What is your favorite thing about traveling on a train?
- If you could, what would you like to ask the engineer?

Schedule starts with S.
The train must be on time.
It's when our ride must start
and end... just like this rhyme!

DEPART
NEW FREEDOM   11:00am
DEPART
GLEN ROCK   11:30am
ARRIVE
HANOVER JUNCTION 11:50am

A schedule is a plan that shows the time when certain events will happen. For example, you may have a daily schedule: the time you get up in the morning, the time you must go to school, the time when you do your homework and go to bed. That schedule helps you stay organized. A train schedule is a plan that shows when a train will leave the station and when it will return. It helps everyone stay on track!

- Why do people have daily schedules?
- How is a train schedule similar to a family schedule?

T is for the trains —

the ones that are quite small.
A model railroad layout
is fun for one and all.

Miniature railroads are smaller models of the much larger trains you see passing through cities and towns. A miniature railroad may include small houses, little buildings, tiny plants and animals, and, of course, an undersized railroad layout. Many people belong to railroad clubs that promote the hobby of model railroading. Be sure to see the model railroad in the NCR station. It's really quite amazing!

- How is a model railroad similar to a real railroad?
- If you could build a model railroad, what would you include?

Uphill starts with **U**.
The train begins a climb.
It needs some extra power
and a little extra time.

If you have ever walked up a hill, you know it's a little harder than walking on flat ground. You need a little more energy and a little more power to get to the top. So does a train. There are several uphill sections on the Northern Central Railway, but the train always has enough power to get up and over these challenges.

- What is the tallest hill or mountain you have climbed?
- Why do you think it is easier for a train to go downhill rather than uphill?

V is for the volunteers
who help in every way.
They make for happy travels
every single day.

You like to help other people, don't you? The volunteers at Northern Central Railway of York like to help people, too. They work in the ticket booth, the gift shop, and on the train. They help make the entire experience enjoyable and safe.

- Why do you think people volunteer to help at Northern Central Railway?
- What is something you could volunteer for in your community?

Whistle starts with **W**—
the sound heard far and wide.
It makes a mighty noise
as we start out on our ride.

A train whistle is a loud signaling device on a locomotive – either steam or diesel. It's an indication that the train is beginning to move along the tracks or that it is approaching a railroad crossing. It also communicates with rail workers and warns others (from a distance) that a train is approaching.

- What do you like most about the sound of a train whistle?
- Why do you think train whistles are so loud?

The crossing has an X—
a sign for me and you.
It tells us: look both ways
for the train that's chugging through.

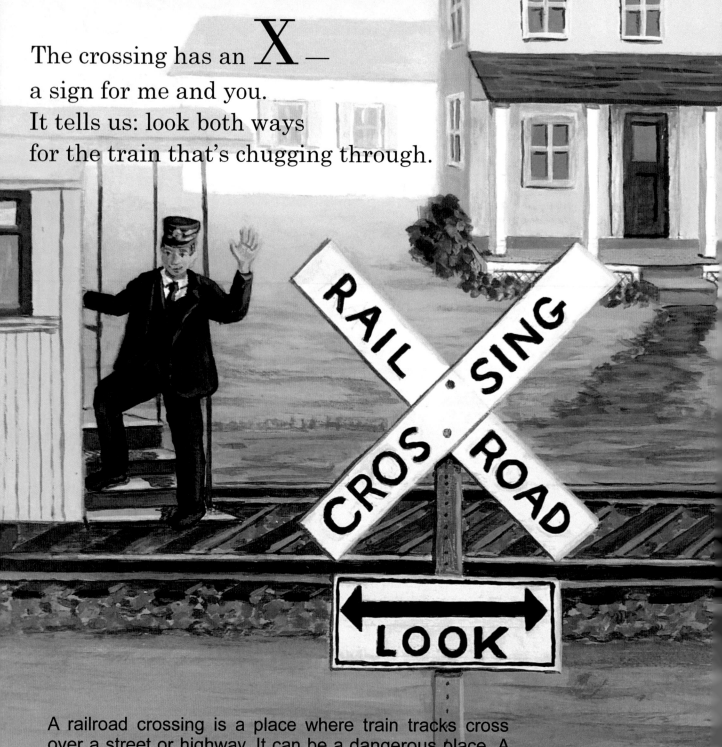

A railroad crossing is a place where train tracks cross
over a street or highway. It can be a dangerous place. A
railroad crossing sign (in the shape of an "X") lets car
drivers know they are approaching some tracks. To be
safe, they need to slow down, stop, and look both ways.

- Why do you think railroad crossings are dangerous places?
- Why do you think it's important for people to look both ways
  when they come to a railroad crossing?

Y is for the Younger Gang — they shoot and rob and run. Be careful with your money... their act is really fun!

During the 1800s, a bunch of outlaws (known as the James – Younger Gang) included the infamous Jesse James and the notorious Younger Brothers. Today, this group (now known as Jesse James and the Younger Gang) includes several men and women who "rob the train" and add a lot of humor to the experience. Passengers are part of every "robbery," so be careful to check your money when you get on board the train.

- Why do you think a "train robbery" might be fun?
- What are some of the fun things you do almost every day?

Z is for a zero
on the front of "17."
Look closely and you'll find it.
Is it silver, gold, or green?

Engine No. 17 (also known as the "William H. Simpson") is Northern Central Railway's steam engine. It is a reproduction of an American Type (4-4-0) locomotive, a type common on North American railroads in the mid to late 19th century. No. 17, however, burns oil instead of wood.

- What do you like most about the look or design of No. 17?
- What would you like to say to the people who built No. 17?

S.T.E.A.M. Activities

There are many exciting things to learn about trains. Listed below are five individual activities for youngsters to try at home or school. These projects use an educational model known as S.T.E.A.M. (**S**cience, **T**echnology, **E**ngineering, **A**rt, and **M**ath). Most important, they offer opportunities that will stimulate discussions, foster creative thinking, develop an appreciation for scientific inquiry, and engage kids in the magic of trains.

SCIENCE

Trains make many sounds. Some of those sounds are high-pitched (a train whistle) and some are low-pithed (the "chug" of the engine). Pitch is the way your brain interprets a sound based on its frequency (vibrations per second). High-pitched sounds are the result of rapid vibrations; low-pitched sounds are the result of slower vibrations.

Get five empty glass bottles (baby food jars, soda pop bottles). All the bottles should be the same size and shape. Invite your child to take one of the bottles, hold it up to her/his lips, and blow across the top of the bottle. Your child will be creating a sound (similar to a train whistle). That's because she/he is making air molecules vibrate. Those vibrations create sound waves.

Now fill each of the five bottles with a different amount of water (1/5 full, 2/5 full, 3/5 full, 4/5 full, and full). Have your child tap each bottle with a metal spoon (several times). Each time a bottle is tapped, the water molecules vibrate and create sound through the water. More water (in a bottle) means slower vibrations and a deeper tone. Less water (in a bottle) means faster vibrations and a higher tone. In other words, the bottle with the most water will have the lowest pitch while the bottle with the least water will have the highest pitch.

Now, when your child listens to the sounds of a train she/he will be able to estimate which ones have a high pitch (fast vibrations) and which ones have a low pitch (slow vibrations).

TECHNOLOGY

Riding the trains of the Northern Central Railway of York is an amazing journey… for kids of all ages. They experience the history of York County, some of a train's engineering challenges, and the ways in which trains operate. Trains open up new worlds of scientific discovery for children. You can help children appreciate the magic of train travel and give them important background experiences by sharing a few YouTube videos produced expressly for youngsters. Here are some favorites:

- ULTIMATE Train Video for Children (4:33)
- Blippi Explores a Steam Train (11:33)
- BIG TRAINS in Action #1 (4:11)
- Steam Trains Galore 5 (23:24)

After viewing, ask children what they saw and heard. Then, read this book aloud – inviting youngsters to imagine they are on a train. Ask them what they learned or what they experienced on their imaginary train ride.

ENGINEERING

In the "old days," steam locomotives needed one essential ingredient in order to run — water! Water was loaded into large boilers and then heated to high temperatures in order to produce the steam necessary to power a steam locomotive. As a result, the railroad built large water towers at strategic places along a railroad line.

When a steam train pulled into a station to unload passengers or freight, it would also fill up with a supply of water.

Children can build their own water towers using just clothespins and craft sticks. Look at the photograph on the left below to see how to connect the clothespins and craft sticks. The photo on the right shows a tower in the process of being constructed. Invite children to begin building their own "water towers." What are some of the challenges they experience? What happens to a "tower" when it gets taller? How could they make their tower stronger?

ART

When children ride an NCR train, invite them to look around for various shapes and designs. At home or at school, invite them to look at various photographs of trains or YouTube videos of railroads. Ask them to keep their eyes open for different shapes, designs, or geometric figures.

Now, invite children to select one of the figures below. Duplicate the selected figure on a sheet of paper. Ask children to use a pencil or marker to turn the figure into a part of a train (e.g. coach car) or something found on the train (e.g. smokestack), or in the train (e.g. conductor's watch). The drawing can be large or small, simple or detailed, or black/white or colored.

MATH

A train has many parts. They must all work together to make sure the train can travel down the track. The chart below has just a few of the many parts on a train:

windows	doors	passenger cars	headlights	engines
wheels	lights	freight cars	ladders	axles
smokestack	roof	whistles	couplings	pistons

Print out several photographs or illustrations of trains from Google Images or Bing Images. Take two dice and roll them. Pick an item from the chart and see if your child can locate that number of items in the image. For example, if you rolled a "3" and a "2" that would equal "5." Let's say you selected the word "windows" from the chart. Can your child find five windows in one of the images? What about "8" wheels? Or, how about "4" doors?

A Little Bit of History

What is now the Northern Central Railway of York was the result of a merger between four different railroads: the Baltimore and Susquehanna Railroad, the York and Maryland Line Railroad, the York and Cumberland Railroad, and the Susquehanna Railroad. The original railroad (the Baltimore and Susquehanna) began in 1828, but it suffered from continuous financial problems and its charter was eventually dissolved. A new charter for the Northern Central Railroad originated in 1854, with operations beginning in 1855. This new rail line was initially established as an alternative to the Tidewater Canal — providing both commercial and passenger transportation along the Susquehanna River.

During the Civil War, the Northern Central Railway was a frequent target of Confederate troops. Telegraph lines were severed, rail joints were destroyed, bridges were burned, and train robberies were a frequent occurrence. In June of 1863, Confederate troops attacked Hanover Junction. They burned the covered bridge over Codorus Creek, as well as the locomotive turntable, and several bridges. They tore up tracks and cut down miles of telegraph poles.

After the Civil War, rail traffic on the line was constant up through WWII. Over the years, diesels replaced steam locomotives. However, the introduction of the Interstate Highway System initiated the decline of the Northern Central. The last regularly scheduled passenger train ran in 1959 and transportation of freight continued to decrease even after the merger (1968) with the New York Central to create the Penn Central.

The penultimate blow to the Northern Central came on June 22, 1972, when Hurricane Agnes dumped 16 inches of rain over the area. Most of the bridges and culverts along the line were destroyed. A series of abandonments, restorations, and take-overs followed. A dinner train operated on the tracks in the 1990s, but eventually went out of business. In 2013, Steam Into History began a tourist excursion railroad from New Freedom to Hanover Junction. Renamed the Northern Central Railway of York, it's an amazing journey through history for everyone.

Fascinating Facts

- Every American president from Abraham Lincoln to Dwight Eisenhower traveled on the Northern Central Railroad. Mark Twain and the Queen of England were also passengers.

- At one time, 88 trains a day passed through Glen Rock. They were primarily freight trains hauling anthracite coal from Williamsport to Baltimore.

- The original name for the station in New Freedom was Summit Station #2. This was because New Freedom is the highest point between York and Baltimore.

- The labor for constructing the railroad was mostly by Irish immigrants who came to the U.S. in the 1830s and 1840s.

- Originally, seven different routes were considered for the railroad tracks. The current one follows Codorus Creek and offers gentle hills along the route.

- The Howard Tunnel (near Seven Valleys) is the second oldest active rail tunnel in the U.S. In operation since 1838, it was a target of Confederate troops during the Civil War. It became part of the National Register of Historic Places in 1995.

- Train stations were placed at 5-mile intervals because the original railroad was designed to be rail cars pulled by draft horses. It was determined that five miles was the distance a team of horses could pull a heavy rail car before needing relief. The stations of Glen Rock and Hanover Junction are exactly five and ten miles from New Freedom.

Dedication

To our granddaughters — Amelia and Lara.
May their travels be full of incredible
adventures and packed with
amazing discoveries!

—Pop-Pop & Grandma

Acknowledgments

This book would not have been possible without the commitment, devotion, and input of numerous people.

Most important — to my wife, Phyllis, an abundance of hugs (and a very special night out) for her superlative illustrations that colorfully and beautifully celebrate the wonder of trains. She is an integral part of this journey...and my life!

I am particularly indebted to Ashley Zimmerman, who initially brought me on board the Northern Central Railway of York. She has been a constant and enthusiastic supporter of the S.T.E.A.M. initiative and her dynamic and wondrous influence is on every page.

To a magnificent NCR crew — Michael J. Patrick, Scott Butcher, Seth Noll, Jeffrey Simpson, Judy Simpson, Rachel Wetzel, and Terri Lehman — all of whom supported and promoted this project from the very beginning. Thank you so much for your engaging camaraderie and your constant passion for education.

A hearty cheer (and a thunderous standing ovation) goes to conductor Barry Larkin whose knowledge of the history of the Northern Central Railway of York is beyond compare! His input and perspective were instrumental in making this book both possible as well as accurate. Indeed, hats off (and lots of "high fives") to the entire NCR organization, who has made this a most marvelous journey through time, traditions, and the magic of trains!

—A.D.F.

About the Author and Illustrator

ANTHONY D. FREDERICKS is Professor Emeritus of Education at York College of PA. He is well-known for his popular and award-winning children's books including *Tall Tall Tree*; *Desert Night, Desert Day*; and *Under One Rock*. Dr. Fredericks is also the Featured Author (2020-2023) for the York County Library System and the Education Consultant for Northern Central Railway of York. When he's not writing, he can be found paddling his kayak on quiet lakes or camping in various Pennsylvania State Parks.

For more information, visit:
www.anthonydfredericks.com

PHYLLIS DISHER FREDERICKS, a professional artist and illustrator, has exhibited her works in oil and acrylics at many regional galleries and museum settings, including the Members Gallery at the Philadelphia Museum of Art and the Whitaker Center for Science and the Arts. She has won numerous awards, including the Rottler Award for Excellence in the Arts. Fredericks is also a retired Adjunct Professor in Art at York College of PA. An active nature lover and advocate, she hikes and camps as often as possible.

For more information, visit:
www.phyllisdisherfredericks.com

ISBN 13: 978-1-64649-149-0
ISBN 10: 1-64649-149-1

Year of the Book
135 Glen Avenue
Glen Rock, PA 17327

Made in the USA
Middletown, DE
28 April 2021